Mel Bay Presents

SONGS OF THE WESTERN FRONTIER

By Jerry Silverman

Cover illustration by Greg Ragland.

Contents

GO WEST

Will You Go Out West?

Where__ is the girl__ who will go out west with me? We'll live in some de-sired__ place, and

hap-py we will be. We'll have a lit-tle cab-in with the ground for a floor, A

dis-tance for a win-dow and a plank for a door. so, Will you go out west,

will you go out west, will you go out west with me? Will you go out west,

4

will you go out west? Oh, say, will you go out west with me?

When I am a-reaping and it looks so much like rain,
She mustn't be afraid for to help get in the grain,
She mustn't be afraid if a-hunting I should go
To chase the wild deer, or to hunt the buffalo.   *Chorus*

I do not care for riches not for beautiful form,
But I want her to be righteous and never raise a storm.
Her hair and her eyes, both they must be,
Now if you know of such a girl, just speak to her for me. *Chorus*

Come all you pretty fair maids and list to what I say,
One year from this present time I'm going far away,
And if I do not find such a girl to be my wife,
I'm going to live a bachelor the rest of my life. *Chorus*

Courtesy, Colorado Historical Society

The Homestead Of The Free

Words by John Greenleaf Whittier

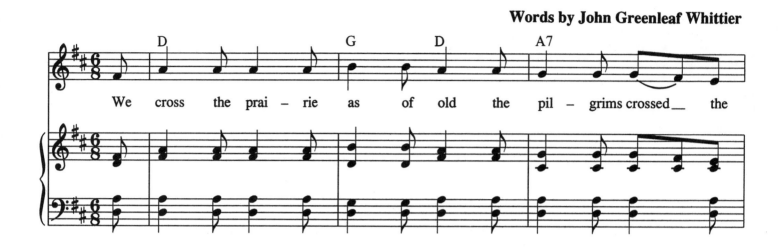

We cross the prai – rie as of old the pil – grims crossed __ the

sea, _____ To __ make the West, as they the East, The

home – stead of ___ the free. _____ The __ home – stead of the

6

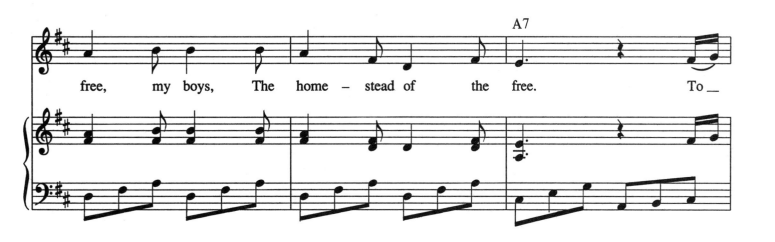

free, my boys, The home – stead of the free. To _

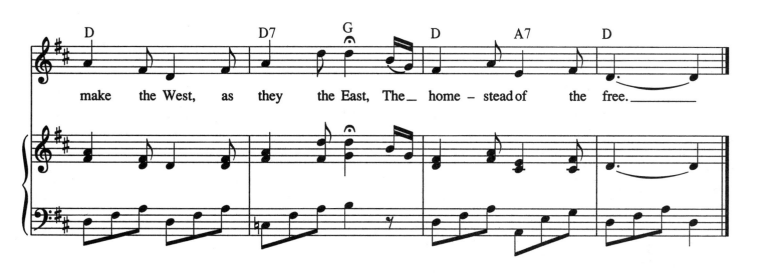

make the West, as they the East, The _ home – stead of the free. _____

We go to rear a wall of men
On freedom's southern line,
And plant beside the cotton bale
The rugged northern pine. *Chorus*

We go to plant her common schools
On distant prairie swells;
And give the Sabbath of the wild
The music of her bells. *Chorus*

Up-bearing, like the ark of old,
The Bible in our van;
We go to test the truth of God
Against the fraud of man. *Chorus*

Hunt The Buffalo

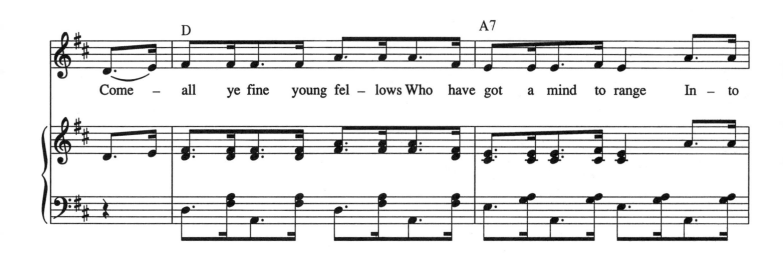

Come – all ye fine young fel – lows Who have got a mind to range In – to

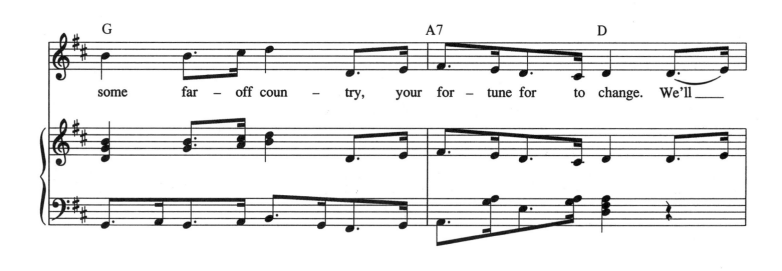

some far – off coun – try, your for – tune for to change. We'll___

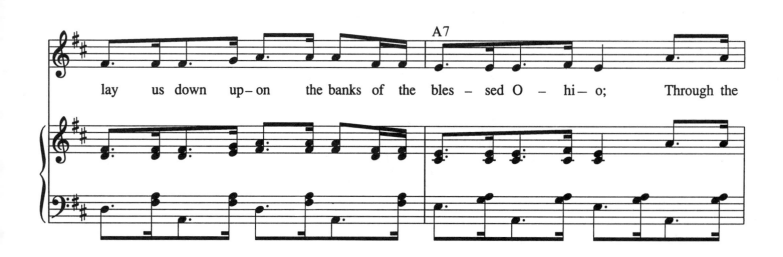

lay us down up – on the banks of the bles – sed O – hi – o; Through the

wild – woods we will wan – der, And we'll hunt the buf – fa – lo.

Come all ye fine young women
Who have got a mind to go.
That you may make us clothing
You can knit and you can sew.
We'll build you fine log cabins
By the blessed O-hi-o;
Through the wildwoods we'll wander,
And we'll hunt the buffalo.

And should the dread wild Indians
By chance to us come near,
We'll all unite together,
And show we have no fear.
We'll bind ourselves together
And strike the fatal blow;
Through the wildwoods we'll wander,
And we'll hunt the buffalo.

Rio Grande

Oh, say were you ev – er in Ri – o Grande? Way_____

_____ oh Ri – o._____ It's there that the riv – er runs

down gold – en sand, And we're bound for the Ri – o Grande.

Chorus

Then, a – way, love,___ a – way._____ Way,_____

oh Ri – o,_____ So fare – ye well,__ my

pret – ty young gal, And we're bound for the Ri – o Grande._____

And goodbye, fare you well, all you ladies of town,
    Way, oh, Rio.
We've left you enough for to buy a silk gown,
    And we're bound for the Rio Grande. *Chorus*

It's pack up your donkey and get under way,
    Way, oh, Rio.
The girls we are leaving can take our half-pay,
    And we're bound for the Rio Grande. *Chorus*

Now, you Bowery ladies, we'd have you to know,
    Way, oh, Rio.
We're bound to the southward, Oh Lord, let us go,
    And we're bound for the Rio Grande. *Chorus*

Santy Anno

We're sail—ing down the riv—er from Liv—er — pool, Heave a—

way, San — ty An—no! _____ A —

round Cape Horn to Fris — co Bay, All___

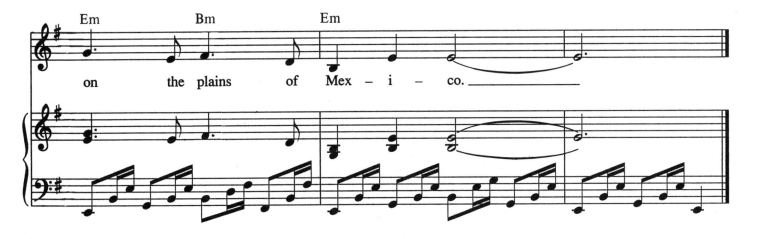

on   the plains   of   Mex – i – co. _____

Chorus So heave her up and away we go,
Heave away, Santy Anno!
Heave her up and away we go,
All on the plains of Mexico.

She's a fast clipper ship and a bully good crew,
Heave away, Santy Anno!
A down-east Yankee for her captain,too,
All on the plains of Mexico. *Chorus*

There's plenty of gold, so I've been told,
Heave away, Santy Anno!
There's plenty of gold, so I've been told,
All on the plains of Mexico. *Chorus*

Back in the days of Forty-Nine,
Heave away, Santy Anno!
Those were the days of the good old times,
All on the plains of Mexico. *Chorus*

When Zacharias Taylor gained the day,
Heave away, Santy Anno!
He made poor Santy run away,
All on the plains of Mexico. *Chorus*

General Scott and Taylor, too,
Heave away, Santy Anno!
Made poor Santy meet his Waterloo,
All on the plains of Mexico. *Chorus*

Santy Anno was a good old man,
Heave away, Santy Anno!
Till he got into war with your Uncle Sam,
All on the plains of Mexico. *Chorus*

When I leave this ship I will settle down,
Heave away, Santy Anno!
And marry a girl named Sally Brown,
All on the plains of Mexico.   *Chorus*

The Utah Iron Horse

Mormon Song

The i – ron horse draws nigh with its smok–y nos–trils high, Eat – ing fire ___ while he graz – eth, Drink–ing wat – er while he blaz – eth. Then the steam forc – es out, Whis – tles loud clear the route; For the i – ron horse is com – ing with a train in his wake.

We have isolated been,
But soon we shall be seen:
Thru this White Mountain region
Folks can learn of our religion
Count each man, many wives,
How they're held in their hives,
And see those dreadful dives,
How they lynch many lives.

If alive we shall be,
Many folks we shall see,
Nobles, lords, flotsam, beggars,
Among us will come the slavers.
Saints will come, sinners too.
We'll have all that we can do,
For this great Union Railroad
It will fetch the devil through.

Courtesy, Colorado Historical Society

My Home's Across The Smoky Mountains

My home's a – cross the Smok–y Moun – tains, My

home's a – cross the Smok–y Moun – tains, My

home's a – cross the Smok–y Moun – tains, And I'll

nev – er get to see you an – y more, more, more, ___ And I'll

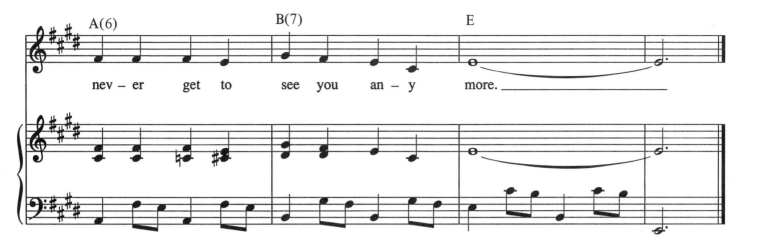

A(6)   B(7)   E

nev – er   get   to   see   you   an – y   more. _____

Good-bye, honey, sugar darling (3)
And I'll never get to see you any more, more, more,
And I'll never get to see you any more.

Rock my honey, feed her candy (3)
And I'll never get to see you any more, more, more,
And I'll never get to see you any more.

I'm going back to the red clay country, (3)
And I'll never get to see you any more, more, more,
And I'll never get to see you any more.

I'd Like To Be In Texas

In a lob – by of a big ho – tel in New York town one
told of plac – es where they'd been and all the sights they'd

day, Sat a bunch of fel – lows tell – ing yarns to
seen, And some

pass the time a – way. They of them praised Chi –

ca – go town, And oth – ers New Or – leans.

To verse 2; then Chorus

In a corner in an old arm chair sat a man whose hair was gray,
He had listened to them longingly, to what they had to say.
They asked him where he'd like to be and his clear old voice did ring:
"I'd like to be in Texas for the round-up in the spring. *Chorus*

They all sat still and listened to each word he had to say;
They knew the old man sitting there had once been young and gay.
They asked him for a story of his life out on the plains,
He slowly then removed his hat and quietly began: *Chorus*

"Oh, I've seen them stampede o'er the hills, when you'd think they'd never stop,
I've seen them run for miles until their leader dropped,
I was foreman on a cow ranch — that's the calling of a king;
I'd like to be in Texas for the round-up in the spring." *Chorus*

Sweet Betsy From Pike

Did you ev – er hear tell of sweet Bet – sy from Pike, Who

crossed the wide prai – ries with her lov – er, Ike; With two yoke of

ox – en and one spot – ted hog, A___ tall shang – hai roos – ter, an old yel – low

dog? Sing___ too – ral – i, oo – ral – i oo – ral – i – ay.

One evening quite early they camped on the
  Platte,
'Twas near by the road on a green shady
  flat;
Where Betsy, quite tired, lay down to
  repose,
While with wonder Ike gazed on his Pike
  County rose. *Chorus*

They stopped at Salt Lake to inquire the
  way,
Where Brigham declared that sweet Betsy
  should stay.
But Betsy got frightened and ran like a
  deer,
While Brigham stood pawing the ground
  like a steer. *Chorus*

Out on the prairie one bright starry night
They broke out the whisky and Betsy got
  tight.
She sang and she shouted and danced o'er
  the plain,
And showed her bare arse to the whole
  wagon train. *Chorus*

The Injuns came down in a wild yelling
  horde,
And Betsy was skeered they would scalp
  her adored.
Behind the front wagon wheel Betsy did
  crawl,
And fought off the Injuns with musket and
  ball. *Chorus*

The Shanghai ran off and their cattle all
  died,
That morning the last piece of bacon was
  fried.
Poor Ike got discouraged and Betsy got mad,
The dog drooped his tail and looked
  wondrously sad. *Chorus*

They soon reached the desert where Betsy
  gave out,
And down in the sand she lay rolling about,
While Ike in great terror looked on in
  surprise,
Saying, "Betsy, get up, you'll get sand in
  your eyes." *Chorus*

The alkali desert was burning and bare,
And Isaac's soul shrank from the death
  that lurked there:
"Dear old Pike County, I'll go back to
  you."
Says Betsy, "You'll go by yourself if you
  do." *Chorus*

They swam the wide rivers and crossed
  the tall peaks,
They camped on the prairie for weeks
  upon weeks.
Starvation and cholera, hard work and
  slaughter,
They reached California spite of hell and
  high water. *Chorus*

One morning they climbed up a very high
  hill,
And with wonder looked down upon old
  Placerville.
Ike shouted and said, as he cast his eyes
  down,
"Sweet Betsy, my darling, we've got to
  Hangtown." *Chorus*

Long Ike and Sweet Betsy attended a dance,
And Ike wore a pair of his Pike County
  pants.
Sweet Betsy was dressed up in ribbons and
  rings,
Says Ike, "You're an angel, but where are
  your wings?" *Chorus*

A miner said, "Betsy, will you dance with
  me?"
"I will, you old hoss, if you don't make too
  free.
But don't dance me hard—do you want to
  know why?
Doggone ye, I'm chock-full of strong
  alkali!" *Chorus*

Long Ike and Sweet Betsy got married, of
  course,
But Ike, getting jealous, obtained a
  divorce.
And Betsy, well satisfied, said with a
  shout,
"Good-bye, you big lummox, I'm glad you
  backed out!" *Chorus*

The Lovely Ohio

Come all ye brisk young fel – lows ___ who have a mind to roam ___ All in some for – eign coun – ter–ee, a long way from home; ___ All in some for – eign coun – ter–ee, a – long with me to go, And we'll set – tle on the banks of the love – ly O – hi – o, We'll

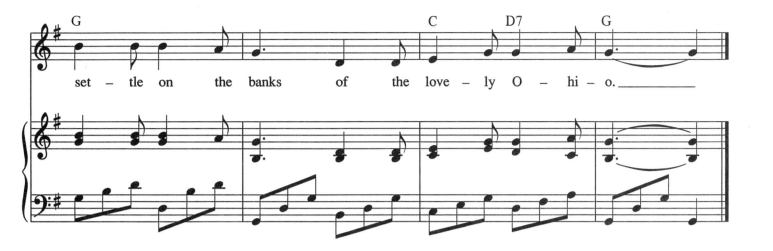

set – tle on the banks of the love – ly O – hi – o. _____

Come all you pretty fair maids, spin us some yarn
To make us some nice clothing to keep ourselves warm.
For you can knit and sew, my loves, while we do reap and mow,
When we settle on the banks of the lovely Ohio. *Chorus*

There are fishes in the river, just fitted for our use.
There's all and lofty sugar cane that will give to us its juice,
There's every kind of game, my boys, also the buck and doe,
When we settle on the banks of the lovely Ohio. *Chorus*

We're Coming, Arkansas

They say there is a stream Where crys – tal wa–ters flow, That –'ll
cure a man sick or well, If he will on – ly go. We're
com – ing, Ar – kan – sas. We're com – ing. Ar – kan – sas. Our
four – horse team will soon be seen On the road to Ar – kan – sas.

The men keep hounds down there,
And hunting is all they care;
The women plough and hoe the corn,
While the men shoot turkey and deer. *Chorus*

The girls are strong down there,
Clean and healthy and gay,
They card and spin from morning 'til night
And dance from night 'til day. *Chorus*

They raise their 'baccer patch,
The women all smoke and chaw,
Eat hog, and hominy and poke for greens
Way down in Arkansas. *Chorus*

The roads are rough down there,
You must take 'um done or raw,
There's rocks and rills and stumps and hills
On the road to Arkansas. *Chorus*

The Sioux Indians

I'll sing you a song, though it may be a sad one, Of tri – als and trou – bles, and where first be – gun. I left my dear kin – dred, my friends, and my home, And we crossed the wide des – erts and moun – tains to roam.

I crossed the Missouri and joined a large train
Which bore us o'er mountain and valley and plain,
And often of evenings out hunting we'd go
To shoot the fleet antelope and the wild buffalo.

We traveled three weeks till we came to the Platte.
And pitched out our tents at the head of a flat;
We'd spread down our blankets on the green grassy ground,
While our horses and oxen were a-grazing around.

While taking refreshments we heard a low yell,
The whoop of Sioux Indians coming up from the dell;
We sprang to our rifles with a flash in each eye.
"Boys," says our brave leader, "we'll fight till we die."

They made a bold dash and came near to our train,
And the arrows fell down just like hail and like rain,
But with our long rifles we fed them cold lead
'Til many a brave warrior around us lay dead.

With our small band, there were just twenty-four,
And of the Sioux Indians there were five hundred or more,
We fought them with courage, we spoke not a word,
'Til the end of the battle that was all that was heard.

We shot their bold Chief at the head of the band,
He died like a warrior with the gun in his hand,
When they saw their full Chief laying dead in his gore,
They whooped and they yelled and we saw them no more.

We hitched up our horses and started our train,
Three more bloody battles this trip on the plain.
And in our last battle three of our brave boys they did fall,
And we left them to rest in a green shady dell.

We traveled by day, guarded camp during night,
Till Oregon's mountains look'd high in their might
Now at Pocahontas beside a clear stream
Our journey has ended in the land of our dream.

Courtesy, Colorado Historical Society

Banks Of The Sacramento

I've been told, On the banks of the Sac — ra — men — to.

O we were the boys to make her go,
With a hoodah, with a hoodah,
Around Cape Horn in the frost and snow,
With a hoodah, hoodah day.   *Chorus*

Around Cape Stiff in seventy days,
With a hoodah, with a hoodah,
Around Cape Stiff is a mighty long ways,
With a hoodah, hoodah day.   *Chorus*

When we was tacking 'round Cape Horn,
With a hoodah, with a hoodah,
I often wished I'd a never been born,
With a hoodah, hoodah day.   *Chorus*

O the mate he whacked me around and around,
With a hoodah, with a hoodah,
And I wished I was home all safe and sound,
With a hoodah, hoodah day.   *Chorus*

O when we got to the Frisco docks,
With a hoodah, with a hoodah,
The girls all were in their Sunday frocks,
With a hoodah, hoodah day.   *Chorus*

California Stage Company

There's no re-spect for youth or age On board of a Cal-i-for-nia stage; But
pull and haul a-bout for seats, As bed-bugs do a-mong the sheets. They__
start-ed out as a thiev-ing line In eight-een hun-dred and for-ty nine. All
op-po-si-tion__ they de-fy, So__ peo-ple must root, hog or die.

You're crowded in with Chinamen,
As fattening hogs are in a pen;
And what will more a man provoke,
Is musty plug tobacco smoke. *Chorus*

The ladies are compelled to sit
With dresses in tobacco spit;
The gentlemen don't seem to care,
But talk on politics and swear. *Chorus*

The dust is deep in summer time,
The mountains very hard to climb;
And drivers often stop and yell,
"Get out all hands, and push - *up hill!*" *Chorus*

The drivers, when they feel inclined,
Will have you walking on behind,
And on your shoulders lug a pole,
To help them through some muddy hole. *Chorus*

They promise, when your fare you pay,
"You'll have to walk but *half* the way";
Then add *aside*, with cunning laugh,
"You'll push and pull the other half!" *Chorus*

They have and will monpolize
The business, 'till the *people rise,*
And send them "kiteing" down below,
To start a line with Bates and Rowe! *Chorus*

Molly Durkin

I'm a da – cint hon – est work – in' man, as you might un – der –
stand, And I'll tell to you the rea – son why I left old I – re –
land. 'Twas Mol – ly Dur – kin did it when she mar – ried Tim O'–
shea, And to keep my heart from break – in; I sailed to A – mer – i – cay.

Chorus

Ar – ragh, Good – bye, Mol – ly Dur – kin, I'm sick and tired of work – in; And my

heart is near – ly brok – en, but no long – er I'll be fooled; And as

sure as my name is Coon – ey, I'm bound for Cal – i – foon – y, And in –

stead of dig – gin' mor – tar I'll be dig – gin' lumps of gold.

Well, I landed in Castle Garden,* sure I met a man named **Burke,**
And he told me remain in New York until he got me work.
But he hasn't got it for me, so tonight I'll tell him plain,
For San Francisco in the morn I'm goin' to take a train. *Chorus*

Well, I'm out in Cal-i-forn-i and my fortune it is made.
I'm a-loaded down with gold and I throw away my pick and spade,
Sail home to dear old Ireland with the Castle out of sight.
And I'll marry Miss O'Kelly, Molly Durkin for to spite. *Chorus*

*Castle Garden was the immigrant reception center in New York before Ellis Island was used.

Courtesy, Colorado Historical Society

34

GOOD TIMES

El-A-Noy

Way down _____ up on the Wa – bash, Such land was nev – er known. If

Ad – am had passed o – ver it, the soil he'd sure – ly own. He'd

think it was the gar – den he'd played in when a boy, And

straight pro – nounce it E – den in the State of El – a – noy.

Chorus

Then move your fam – 'ly west – ward, Good health you will en – joy, And rise to wealth and hon – or in the State of El – a – noy.

'Twas here the Queen of Sheba came,
With Solomon of old,
With an ass-load of spices,
Pomegranates and fine gold;
And when she saw this lovely land,
Her heart was filled with joy,
Straightway she said: "I'd like to be
A Queen in El-a-noy." *Chorus*

She's bounded by the Wabash,
The Ohio and the Lakes,
She's crawfish in the swampy lands,
The milk-sick and the shakes;
But these are slight diversions
And take not from the joy
Of living in this garden land,
The State of El-a-noy. *Chorus*

Away up in the northward,
Right on the border line,
A great commercial city,
Chicago, you will find.
Her men are all like Abelard,
Her women like Heloise;
All honest virtuous people,
For they live in El-a-noy. *Chorus*

37

The Kinkaiders

Moses P. Kinkaid, Congressman from the Sixth District in Nebraska, 1903-1913, introduced a bill for 640-acre homesteads and was hailed as a benefactor of the sand hills region.

The corn we raise is our delight,
The melons, too, are out of sight.
Potatoes grown are extra fine
And can't be beat in any clime. *Chorus*

The peaceful cows in pastures dream
And furnish us with golden cream.
So I shall keep my Kinkaid home,
And never far away shall roam. *Chorus*

Final Chorus:
Then let us all with hearts sincere
Thank him for what has brought us here,
And for the homestead law he made,
This noble Moses P. Kinkaid. *Chorus*

Courtesy, Colorado Historical Society

Home On The Range

Words by Higley Brewster
Music by Daniel E. Kelly

40

How often at night when the heavens are bright
With the light from the glittering stars,
Have I stood there amazed and asked as I gazed,
If their glory exceeds that of ours. *Chorus*

Where the air is so pure, the zephyrs so free,
The breezes so balmy and light,
That I would not exchange my home on the range
For all of the cities so bright. *Chorus*

Oh, I love those wild flow'rs in this dear land of ours,
The curlew, I love to hear scream,
And I love the white rocks and the antelope flocks,
That graze on the mountaintops green. *Chorus*

Root, Hog Or Die

I'm a lone-ly bull – whack-er on the Red Cloud Line, I can

lick an – y son-of-a-gun can yoke an ox of mine.

If I can catch him,___ you bet I will or try,___ I'll___

lick him with an ox – bow: Root, hog or die.

Well, it's out upon the road
With a very heavy load,
With a very awkward team
And a very muddy road,
You may whip and you may holler,
If you cuss it's on the sly,
Then it's whack the cattle on, boys:
Root, hog or die.

Now it's out upon the road
These sights are t'be seen,
The antelope and buffalo
The prairie all s'green,
The antelope and buffalo,
The rabbit jumps s'high,
Then it's whack the cattle on, boys:
Root, hog or die.

Now every day at twelve
There's something for to do,
If there's nothing else,
There's a pony for to shoe;
I'll throw him down, boys,
Still I'll make him lie,
Little pig, big pig:
Root, hog or die.

Now perhaps you'd like to know, boys,
What we have to eat,
A little piece of bread
And a little dirty meat,
A little black coffee
And whisky on the sly,
It's whack the cattle on, boys:
Root, hog or die.

There's hard times on Bitter Creek
Never can be beat,
It was root, hog, or die
Under every wagon sheet;
We cleaned up all the Injuns,
Drank all the alkali,
And it's whack the cattle on, boys:
Root, hog or die.

There was good times in Salt Lake
I never can pass by,
That's where I met her,
My China girl called Wi.
She could smile, she could chuckle,
She could roll her hog-eye,
Then it's whack the cattle on, boys:
Root, hog or die.

O I'm a-goin' home
Bull-whackin' for to spurn,
I ain't got a nickel,
And I don't give a durn.
'Tis when I meet a purdy gal
You bet I will or try,
I'll whack her with my ox-bow:
Root, hog or die.

43

Shenandoah

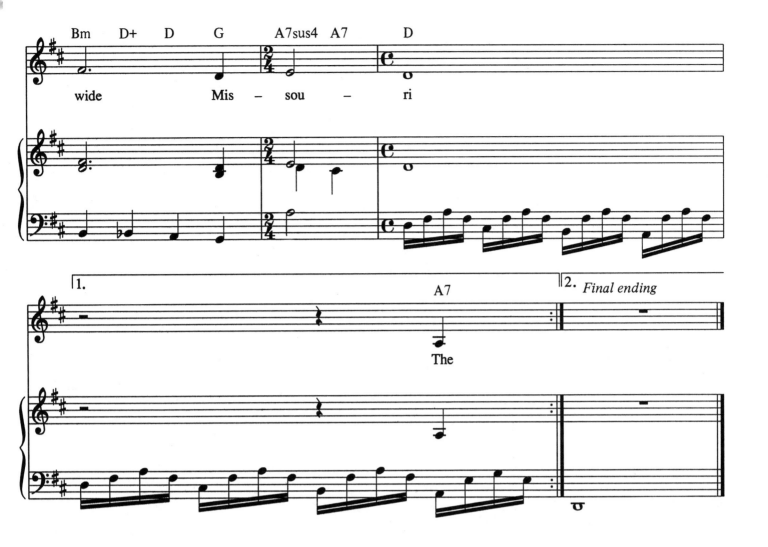

The white man loved the Indian maiden,
  Away, you rolling river,
With notions his canoe was laden.   *Chorus*

O, Shenandoah, I love your daughter,
  Away, you rolling river,
I'll take her 'cross the rolling water.   *Chorus*

O, Shenandoah, I'm bound to leave you,
  Away, you rolling river,
O, Shenandoah, I'll not deceive you.   *Chorus*

Cripple Creek

I got a gal at the head of the creek,

Go up to see her 'bout the mid – dle of the week.

Kiss her on the mouth, just as sweet as an – y wine.

Wraps her – self a – round me like a sweet per – ta – ter vine.

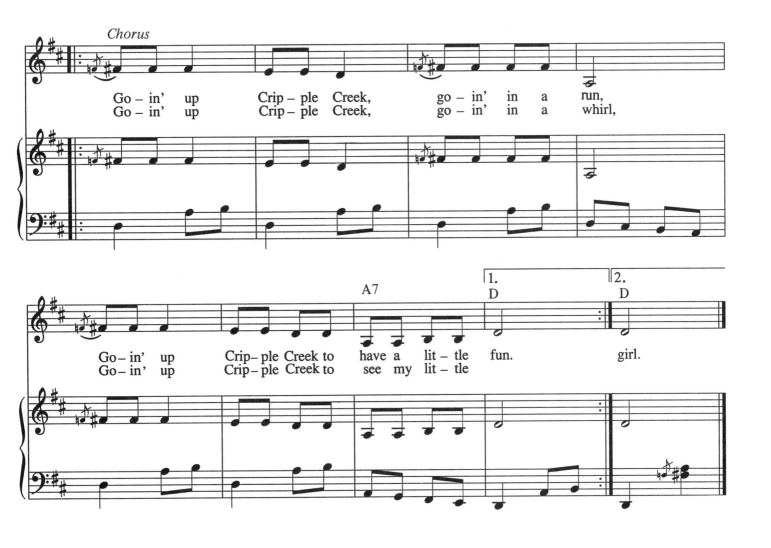

Chorus

Go – in' up Crip – ple Creek, go – in' in a run,
Go – in' up Crip – ple Creek, go – in' in a whirl,

Go – in' up Crip – ple Creek to have a lit – tle fun.
Go – in' up Crip – ple Creek to see my lit – tle

1. girl.
2. fun.

Girls on the Cripple Creek 'bout half grown,
Jump on a boy like a dog on a bone.
Roll my britches up to my knees,
I'll wade old Cripple Creek when I please. *Chorus*

Cripple Creek's wide and Cripple Creek's deep,
I'll wade old Cripple Creek afore I sleep,
Roads are rocky and the hillside's muddy
And I'm so drunk that I can't stand steady. *Chorus*

Courtesy, Colorado Historical Society

The Ox-Driving Song

Chorus:
To my roll, to my roll, to my ride-e-o,
To my roll, to my roll, to my ride-e-o,
To my ride-e-o, to my ru-de-o,
To my roll, to my roll, to my ride-e-o.

On the fourteenth day of October-o,
I hitched my team in order-o.
To drive to the hills of Saludio.
To my roll, to my roll, to my ride-e-o. *Chorus*

When I got there the hills were steep,
A tender-hearted person'd weep
To hear me cuss and pop my whip,
To see my oxen pull and slip. *Chorus*

When I get home I'll have revenge,
I'll land my family among my friends.
I'll bid adieu to the whip and line,
And drive no more in the wintertime. *Chorus*

49

The Gal I Left Behind Me

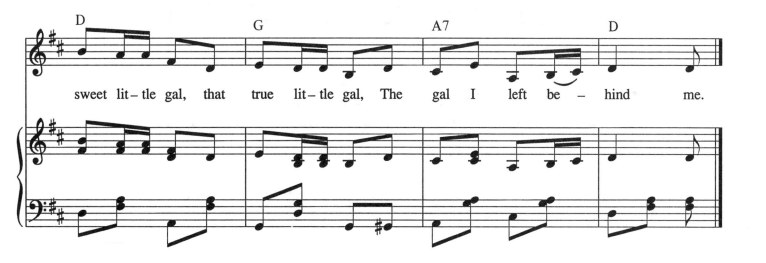

sweet lit–tle gal, that true lit–tle gal, The gal I left be – hind me.

The wind did blow, the rain did fall,
The hail did fall and blind me.
I thought of the gal, that sweet little gal,
The gal I left behind me. *Chorus*

If ever I get off the trail
And the Indians they don't find me,
I'll make my way straight back again
To the gal I left behind me. *Chorus*

When we sold out I took the train,
I knew where I would find her.
When I got back we had a smack,
And that was no golderned liar. *Chorus*

Tying A Knot In The Devil's Tail

They took their horses and their runnin' irons,
And maybe a dog or two,
And they 'lowed they'd brand all the long-eared calves
That came within their view.

Well, many a long-eared dogie
That didn't hush up by day,
Had his long ears whittled and his old hide scorched
In a most artistic way.

Then one fine day said Buster Jiggs,
As he throwed his cigo down:
"I'm tired of cow biography
And I 'lows I'm goin' to town."

They saddles up and they hits them a lope,
Fer it weren't no sight of a ride,
An' them was the days when an old cow hand
Could oil up his old insides.

They starts her out at the Kentucky bar,
At the head of the whisky row,
And they winds her up at the Depot House,
Some forty drinks below.

They sets her up and turns her around
And goes her the other way,
And to tell you the Lord forsaken truth,
Them boys got drunk that day.

Well, as they was a-headin' back to camp,
And packin' a pretty good lead,
Who should they meet but the Devil himself,
Come prancin' down the road.

Now the Devil he said, "You cowboy skunks,
You better go hunt your hole,
'Cause I come up from the hell's rim-rock
To gather in your souls."

Said Buster Jiggs: "Now we're just from town,
An' feelin' kind o' tight,
And you ain't gonna get no cowboy souls
Without some kind of a fight."

So he punched a hole in his old throw-rope,
And he slings her straight and true,
And he roped the Devil right around the horns,
He takes his dallies* true.

Old Sandy Bob was a reata-man**
With his rope all coiled up neat,
But he shakes her out and he builds him a loop,
And he roped the Devil's hind feet.

They threw him down on the desert ground,
While the irons was a-gettin' hot,
They cropped and swallow-forked his ears,
And branded him up a lot.

And they pruned him up with a dehorning saw,
And knotted his tail for a joke,
Rode off and left him bellowing there,
Necked up to a lilac-jack oak.

Well, if you ever travel in the Sierra peaks
And you hear one helluva wail,
You'll know it's nothin' but the Devil himself,
Raisin' hell about the knots in his tail.

*dallies—turns of the rope around the saddle horn
**reata—lasso

The Old Chisholm Trail

Well, come a – long, boys, and lis – ten to my tale, And I'll

tell you of my trou – bles on the old Chis – holm Trail. Come a ti yi yip – pee, yip – pee

yay, yip – pee yay, Come a ti – yi yip – pee, yip – pee yay.

I started up the trail October twenty-third.
I started up the trail with the 2-U herd. *Chorus*

I jumped in the saddle and grabbed a-holt the horn,
Best durn cowboy ever was born. *Chorus*

I'm up in the morning before daylight
And before I sleep, the moon shines bright. *Chorus*

It's bacon and beans 'most every day,
I'd as soon been a-eating prairie hay. *Chorus*

Cloudy in the east and it looks like rain,
And my damned old slicker's in the wagon again. *Chorus*

Wind began to blow — rain began to fall,
It looked, by grab, like we was gonna lose 'em all. *Chorus*

A heifer went loco and the boss said, "Kill it."
I shot it in the arse with the handle of a skillet. *Chorus*

I went to the boss to draw my roll.
He had me figgered out nine dollars in the hole. *Chorus*

So me and the boss, we had a little chat.
I hit him in the face with my big slouch hat. *Chorus*

So the boss said to me, "I'm gonna fire you —
And not only you but the whole damn crew." *Chorus*

Well, I'm going back home to draw my money,
Going back home to see my honey. *Chorus*

On a ten-dollar hoss and a forty-dollar saddle,
I'm a-going to punch them Texas cattle. *Chorus*

Well, my feet are in the stirrup and my saddle's in the sky,
And I'll quit punching cows in the Sweet Bye and Bye. *Chorus*

Courtesy, Colorado Historical Society

55

Git Along, Little Dogies

As I was a – walk – in' one morn – ing for pleas – ure, I
spied a cow – punch – er a – stroll – in' a – long. His hat was throwed
back and his spurs were a jin – glin', And as he ap – proached he was
sing – ing this song. Whoop – ee ti yi yo, Git a –

It's early in the spring that we round up
    the dogies,
We mark them and brand them and bob
    off their tails;
We round the horses, load up the chuck
    wagon,
And then throw the dogies upon the long
    trail. *Chorus*

Your mother was raised away down in
    Texas,
Where the jimpson weed and sand-burrs
    grow,
Now we'll fill you up on prickly pear and
    cactus,
Till you are all ready for the trail to
    Idaho. *Chorus*

Oh, you'll be soup for Uncle Sam's soldiers,
It's, "Beef, more beef," I hear them cry.
Git along, git along, git along little dogies,
You'll be beef steers by and by. *Chorus*

57

My Love Is A Rider

The first time I met him 'twas early in spring;
He was riding a bronco, a high-headed thing.
He tipped me a wink as he gaily did go,
For he wished me to notice his bucking bronco.

The next time I saw him 'twas sometime that fall,
Swinging the girls at Tomlinson's hall.
He laughed and he talked as we danced to and fro,
And promised he'd never ride on another bronco.

He made me some presents, among them a ring.
The return that I made him was a far better thing;
'Twas a young maiden's heart, I'd have you all know;
He'd won it by riding his bucking bronco.

My love has a gun, and that gun he can use,
But he's quit his gun fighting as well as his booze;
And he's sold him his saddle, his spurs, and his rope,
And there's no more cow-punching, and that's what I hope.

Listen all you young maidens, where'er you reside,
Ride shy of the cowboy who swings the raw-hide.
He'll court you and pet you and leave you and go
Up the trail in the spring on his bucking bronco.

I Ride An Old Paint

I ride an old paint,___ I lead an old dan,___ I'm goin' to Mon – tan – a to throw the hou – li – han. They feed in the cou – lees, they wa – ter in the draw; Their tails are all mat – ted, their backs are all raw.

Ride a – round, lit – tle do – gies, Ride a – round ____ them_ slow, For the fier – y and snuf – fy are rar – in' to go.

Old Bill Jones had two daughters and a song,
One went to college, the other went wrong.
His wife got killed in a pool-room fight,
But still he keeps singing from morning 'til
  night.
Chorus

I've worked in the city, worked on the farm,
And all I've got to show is the muscle in my
  arm.
Patches on my pants, callous on my hand,
And I'm goin' to Montana to throw the houlihan.
Chorus

When I die, don't bury me at all.
Put me on my pony and lead him from his stall.
Tie my bones to his back, turn our faces to the
  west,
And we'll ride the prairie that we love the best.
Chorus

61

Courtesy, Colorado Historical Society

Red River Valley

Won't you think of this valley you're leaving,
Oh, how lonely, how sad it will be,
Oh, think of the fond heart you're breaking,
And the grief you are causing me.

From this valley they say you are going,
When you go may your darling go, too?
Would you leave her behind unprotected
When she loves no other but you?

I have promised you, darling, that never
Will a word from my lips cause you pain;
And my life, it will be yours forever,
If you only will love me again.

Zebra Dun

We was camped on the plains, at the head of Cim – ma – ron, When a –
long comes a stran – ger, and stops to ar – gue some. Well, he
looks so ver – y fool – ish, we be – gins to look a – round, For we
think he is a green – horn, and just es – caped from town.

We asks if he had had a feed, he hadn't
   had a smear,
So we opens up the chuck box and forks
   him out a share;
He took a cup of coffee, some biscuit
   and some beans,
And then begins to settle down and talk
   of foreign kings and queens.

And all about the Spanish War, and
   a-fighting on the seas,
With pistols big as muley steers, and
   rifles big as trees,
And about old Paul Jones, that mean,
   fightin' son-of-a-gun;
He says he was the rankest cuss that
   ever pulled a gun.

Such an educated fellow, his thoughts
   just come in herds,
And every livin' sentence, boys, had
   ten jaw-breaking words;
He just keeps on a-talking, boys, till
   he makes us all damn sick,
And we begins to look around just how
   to play a trick.

He said that he had lost his job upon
   the Sante Fe,
And he's a-goin' across the plains to
   strike the old F. D.;
He didn't say how come it, some
   trouble with the boss,
And asks if he can borrow a nice fat
   saddle horse.

This tickles all the boys to death, they
   laughs right up their sleeves,
We'll lend you a horse just as fresh and
   fat as you please;
Well, Shorty grabs the lariat and he
   ropes the zebra dun,
And the boys they all gathers 'round and
   a-waitin' for the fun.

Well, old dunny was a rocky outlaw that
   had growed so awful wild,
That he could paw the moon every jump
   there for a mile;
Old dunny stood right still, as if he did
   not know,
Until we gets him saddled up and ready
   for the show.

When the stranger hits the saddle, well
   old dunny quits the earth,
He travels right straight up for all that
   he was worth;
A-pitchin' and a-squealin' and a-havin'
   wall-eyed fits,
His hind feet perpendicular, his front
   feet in the bits.

We could see them snowy mountain
   tops under dunny every jump,
But that slicker he has growed there
   just like the camel's hump;
The stranger he just perched there
   and curled his black mustache,
Just like some summer boarder, boys,
   a-waitin' for his hash.

He thumps him in the shoulders and he
   spurs him when he whirls,
To show us earthbound punchers that he
   was the top wolf of the world;
When the stranger had dismounted once
   more upon the ground,
We knowed he was the salty dog and
   not no boy from town.

The boss, who was a-standin' 'round
   and a-watchin' of the show,
Walks right up to the stranger and says:
   "You need not go.
If you can use the catch rope like you
   rode old zebra dun,
You're the hand I'm lookin' for since
   the year of one."

Well, he sure could use the catch rope
   and he didn't do it slow,
He sure could forefoot 'em ten times
   there in a row;
And when the herd stampeded he was
   always on the spot
And he sets them critters millin' like
   the boilin' of a pot.

Sung to last 4 measures
There is one thing and a sure thing
That I have learned since I've been
   born,
Every educated fellow, boys,
Ain't no damn plumb greenhorn.

Acres Of Clams

For one who gets riches by mining,
Perceiving that hundreds grow poor,
I made up my mind to try farming,
The only pursuit that is sure.

Chorus: The only pursuit that is sure, (2)
              I made up my mind to try farming,
              The only pursuit that is sure.

So, rolling my grub in a blanket,
I left all my tools on the ground.
And I started one morning to shank it
For the country they call Puget Sound.

Chorus: For the country. . .

Arriving flat broke in midwinter,
The ground was enveloped in fog;
And covered all over with timber
Thick as hair on the back of a dog.

Chorus: Thick as hair. . .

When I looked at the prospects so gloomy
The tears trickled over my face;
And I thought that my travels had brought me
To the end of the jumping-off place.

Chorus: to the end. . .

I staked me a claim in the forest
And set myself down to hard toil.
For two years I chopped and I struggled,
But I never got down to the soil.

Chorus: But I never. . .

I tried to get out of the country,
But poverty forced me to stay.
Until I became an old settler,
Then nothing could drive me away.

Chorus: Then nothing. . .

And now that I'm used to the country,
I think that if man ever found
A place to live easy and happy,
That Eden is on Puget Sound.

Chorus: That Eden. . .

No longer the slave of ambition,
I laugh at the world and its shams;
As I think of my happy condition,
Surrounded by acres of clams.

Chorus: Surrounded by acres. . .

Days Of Forty-Nine

I'm old Tom Moore from the bum - mer's shore, In the good old gold - en
call me a bum-mer and a gin sot too, But what cares I for

day. They praise?

I wan - der a - round from

town ___ to town, Just like a rov - ing sign; And the

peo - ple all say, "There goes Tom Moore, of the days of for - ty - nine,"

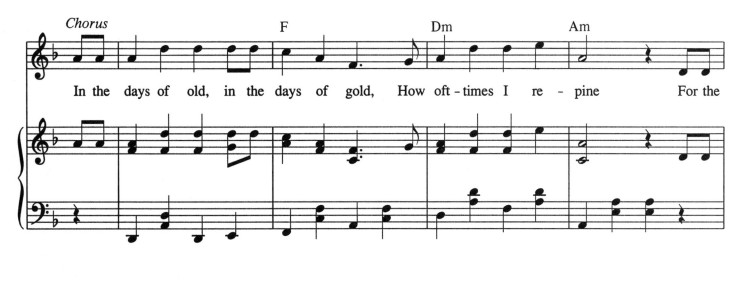

In the days of old, in the days of gold, How oft - times I re - pine For the

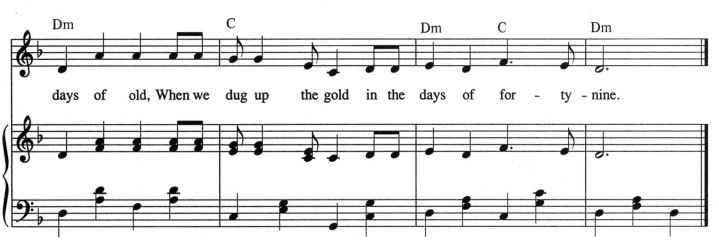

days of old, When we dug up the gold in the days of for - ty - nine.

My comrades they all loved me well,
A jolly, saucy crew,
A few hard cases I will admit,
Though they were brave and true;
Whatever the pinch, they ne'er would flinch,
They never would fret or whine,
Like good old bricks, they stood the kicks
In the days of forty-nine. *Chorus*

There was old Lame Jess, a hard old cuss,
Who never did repent;
He never was known to miss a drink
Or ever spend a cent;
But old Lame Jess, like all the rest,
To death he did resign,
And in his bloom went up the flume
In the days of forty-nine. *Chorus*

There was Poker Bill, one of the boys,
Who was always in for a game,
Whether he lost or whether he won,
To him it was all the same;
He would ante up and draw his cards
He would go you a hatful blind,
In the game with death Bill lost his breath
In the days of forty-nine. *Chorus*

There was New York Jake, the butcher's boy,
He was always getting tight,
And every time that he'd get full
He was spoiling for a fight;
Then Jake rampaged against a knife
In the hands of old Bob Sine;
And over Jake they held a wake
In the days of forty-nine. *Chorus*

There was Ragshag Bill from Buffalo
I never will forget,
He would roar all day and roar all night,
And I guess he's roaring yet;
One night he fell in a prospect hole
In a roaring bad design;
And in that hole he roared out his soul
In the days of forty-nine. *Chorus*

Of all the comrades that I've had
There's none that's left to boast;
And I'm left alone in my misery
Like some poor wandering ghost;
And as I pass from town to town
They call me the rambling sign,
"There goes Tom Moore, a bummer shore,
Of the days of forty-nine." *Chorus*

Courtesy, National Park Service

HARD TIMES

Abilene

Sit alone every night,
Watch the trains roll out of sight,
Don't I wish they were carrying me
To Abilene, my Abilene.

Crowded city — ain't nothin' free;
Ain't nothin' in this crowd for me,
Wish to my God that I could be
In Abilene, my Abilene.

Repeat first verse

Billy The Kid

When Billy the Kid was a very young lad,
In old Silver City he went to the bad.
Way out in the West with a gun in his hand,
At the age of twelve years he killed his first man.

Young Mexican maidens play guitars and sing
Songs about Billy, their boy bandit king,
How there's a young man who had reached his sad end—
Had a notch on his pistol for twenty-one men.

It was on the same night when poor Billy died,
He said to his friends, "I'm not satisfied.
There are twenty-one men I have put bullets through—
Sheriff Pat Garritt must make twenty-two."

Now this is how Billy the Kid met his fate,
The bright moon was shining the hour was late.
Shot down by Pat Garritt who once was his friend,
The young outlaw's life had now reached its sad end.

Now there's many a lad with a face fine and fair,
Who starts out in life with a chance to be square,
But just like poor Billy they wander astray,
They lose their life in the very same way.

The Wyoming Nester

"You've homesteaded all of this country,
Where the slicks and the mavericks did roam;
You've driven me far from my country,
Far from my birthplace and home.

"The cattle are still getting thinner,
And the ranches are shorter on men,
But I've got me a full quart of whisky,
And nearly a full quart of gin.

"You have taken up all of the water,
And all of the land that's nearby" —
And he took a big drink from his bottle
Of good old '99 rye.

He rode far into the evening,
His limbs at last had grown tired.
He shifted himself in his saddle,
And he slowly hung down his head.

His saddle he used for a pillow;
His blanket he used for a bed.
As he lay himself down for a night's slumber,
These words to himself he then said:

"I'm leaving Wyoming forever,
This land and the home of my birth,
It fills my heart with sorrow,
But it fills your heart with mirth."

Courtesy, Colorado Historical Society

Dakota Land

We've reached the land of des – ert sweet, where noth – ing grows for man to eat. The wind it blows with fev - 'rish heat A – cross the plains so hard to beat. *Chorus* O, Da - ko - ta land, sweet Da - ko - ta land, As on thy fier - y soil I stand, I

look a-cross the plains And won-der why it nev - er rains, Till

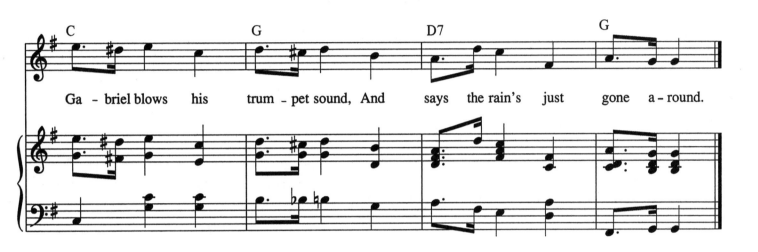

Ga – briel blows his trum – pet sound, And says the rain's just gone a-round.

We've reached the land of hills and stones
Where all is strewn with buffalo bones.
O buffalo bones, bleached buffalo bones,
I seem to hear your sighs and moans. *Chorus*

We have no wheat, we have no oats,
We have no corn to feed our shoats;
Our chickens are so very poor
They beg for crumbs outside the door. *Chorus*

Our horses are of bronco race;
Starvation stares them in the face.
We do not live, we only stay;
We are too poor to get away. *Chorus*

The Boll Weevil

Oh, The boll weev - il is a lit - tle black bug, Come from Mex - i - co, They say. Come all the way to Tex - as, Just a - look - in' for a place to stay. Just a - look - in' for a home, Just a - look in' for a home, Just a - look - in' for a

The first time I seen the boll weevil,
He was sitting on the square.
The next time I seen the boll weevil,
He had all his family there,
Just a-lookin' for a home, just a-lookin' a home.(2)

The farmer said to the weevil,
"What makes your face so red?"
The weevil said to the farmer,
"It's wonder I ain't dead,"
Just a-lookin' for a home, just a-lookin' for a home.(2)

The farmer took the boll weevil,
And he put him in hot sand.
The weevil said, "This is mighty hot,
But I'll stand it like a man,
This'll be my home, this'll be my home." (2)

The farmer took the boll weevil,
And he put him in a lump of ice.
The boll weevil said to the farmer,
"This is mighty cool and nice,
This'll be my home, this'll be my home." (2)

The farmer took the boll weevil,
And he put him in the fire.
The boll weevil said to the farmer,
"This is just what I desire,
This'll be my home, this'll be my home." (2)

The boll weevil said to the farmer,
"You better leave me alone;
I ate up all your cotton,
And I'm starting on your corn,
I'll have a home, I'll have a home." (2)

The merchant got half the cotton,
The boll weevil got the rest.
Didn't leave the farmer's wife
But one old cotton dress,
And it's full of holes, and it's full of holes. (2)

The farmer said to the merchant,
"We're in an awful fix;
The boll weevil ate all the cotton up
And left us only sticks,
We got no home, we got no home." (2)

The farmer said to the merchant,
"We ain't made but one bale,
And before we'll give you that one,
We'll fight and go to jail,
We'll have a home, we'll have a home." (2)

And if anybody should ask you
Who was it sang this song,
It was the poor old farmer
With all but his blue jeans gone,
A-looking for a home. (2)

Courtesy, New York Public Library Picture Collection

79

Buffalo Skinners

I found myself in Texas in the spring of eighty-three,
When a well-known famous drover come a-walking up to me,
Saying, "How do you do, young feller, and how would you like to go
And spend a summer pleasant on the trail of the buffalo?"

Well, me being out of work right then to the drover I did say,
"This going out on the buffalo range depends upon your pay.
But if you will pay good wages, transportation to and fro,
I think I might go with you to the range of the buffalo."

"Of course I'll pay good wages, and transportation, too,
If you'll agree to work for me until the season's through.
But if you should grow weary and decide to run away,
You'll starve to death out on the trail and also lose your pay."

With all this flattering talking he signed up quite a train.
Some ten or twelve in number - some able-bodied men.
Our trip it was a pleasant one as we hit the westward road,
And then we crossed old Boggy Creek in old New Mexico.

Well, there our pleasures ended and our troubles all begun.
A lightning storm did hit us and made our cattle run.
Got all full of stickers from the cactus that did grow,
And outlaws waiting to pick us off on the trail of the buffalo.

Well, the working season ended and the drover would not pay.
"You all have drunk too much. You're all in debt to me!"
But the cowboys never had heard of such a thing as the bankrupt law,
So we left that drover's bones to bleach on the trail of the buffalo.

81

The Farmer Is The Man

When the farm - er comes to town, with his wag - on brok - en
on - ly look and see, Then I think you will a -

down, } Oh the farm - er is the man who feeds them
gree, }

all. _____ If you'll all, _____ The

farm - er is the man, _____ The farm - er is the man.

When the lawyer hangs around, while the butcher cuts a pound,
Oh, the farmer is the man who feeds them all.
And the preacher and the cook go a-strolling by the brook.
Oh, the farmer is the man who feeds them all.

The farmer is the man, the farmer is the man,
Lives on credit till the fall;
With the int' rest rate so high, it's a wonder he don't die,
For the mortgage man's the one who gets it all.

The Dreary Black Hills

The road-house in Cheyenne is filled ev-'ry night With ___ loaf-ers and bum-mers of most ev-'ry plight. On their backs is no clothes, in their pock-ets no bills, Each day they keep start-ing for the drear-y Black Hills

Chorus:
Don't go away, stay at home if you can,
Stay away from that city they call it Cheyenne,
Where the blue waters roll, and Comanche Bills,
They will lift up your hair, on the dreary Black Hills.

I got to Cheyenne, no gold could I find,
I thought of the lunch route I'd left far behind;
Through rain, hail, and snow, frozen plumb to the gills,
They call me the orphan of the dreary Black Hills. *Chorus*

Kind friend, to conclude, my advice I'll unfold,
Don't go to the Black Hills a-hunting for gold;
Railroad speculators their pockets you'll fill
By taking a trip to those dreary Black Hills.

Final Chorus:
Don't go away, stay at home if you can,
Stay away from that city, they call it Cheyenne,
For old Sitting Bull or Comanche Bills
They will take off your scalp on the dreary Black Hills.

Courtesy, Colorado Historical Society

The Tex-i-an Boys

When they come a-courting, I'll tell you what they wear:
An old leather coat all patched and bare,
An old straw hat more brim than crown,
And a pair of dirty socks they've wore the winter 'round. (2)

When he comes in, first thing you hear,
"Madam, has your daddy killed a deer?"
And the next thing he says when he sits down,
"Madam, the johnnycake's too damn brown."   (2)

They will take you out on a live-oak hill,
And love you there against your will.
Love you on the prairie and forget you on the plains,
For that is the way with the Tex-i-ans.   (2)

Brandy is brandy any way you mix it,
A Tex-i-an's a Tex-i-an any way you fix it.
When other good folks have all gone to bed,
The Devil is a-working in the Tex-i-an's head.   (2)

Courtesy, Colorado Historical Society

Cole Younger

I am a not – ed high – way – man, _____ Cole
rob – bing of the North – field Bank, _____ The

Youn – ger is my name. _____ My
same I can't de – ny. _____ For

crimes and dep – re – da – tions _____ Have
now I am a pris – 'ner, _____ In

brought my friends ___ to shame. _____ The ___
Still – wa – ter Jail ___ I lie. _____ ___

1.
2.

'Tis of a bold high robbery, a story I will tell,
Of a California miner who unto us fell,
We robbed him of his money and bid him go his way,
For which I will be sorry until my dying day.

And then we started homeward, when brother Bob did say,
"Now, Cole, we'll buy fast horses and on them ride away;
We'll ride to avenge our father's death and try to win the prize,
We'll fight those anti-guerillas until the day we die."

And then we rode towards Texas, that good old Lone Star state,
But on Nebraska's prairies the James boys we did meet,
With knives and guns and pistols we all sat down to play,
A-drinkin' of good whisky, boys, to pass the time away.

A Union Pacific railway train was the next we did surprise,
And the crimes done by our bloody hands bring tears into my
  eyes,
The engineer and the fireman killed, the conductor escaped alive,
And now their bones lie moldering beneath Nebraska's skies.

Then we saddled horses, northwestward we did go,
To the God-forsaken country called Minnesot-i-o,
I had my eye on the Northfield Bank, when brother Bob did say,
"Now, Cole, if you undertake the job, you'll surely rue the day."

But I stationed out my pickets and up to the bank did go,
And there upon the counter I struck my fatal blow.
"Just hand us over your money and make no further delay,
We are the famous Younger boys, we spend no time in play."

The cashier, being as true as steel, refused our noted band,
'Twas Jesse James that pulled the trigger that killed this noble
  man.
We run for life, for death was near, four hundred on our trail,
We soon were overtaken, and landed safe in jail.

I am a noted highwayman, Cole Younger is my name,
My crimes and depredations have brought my name to shame,
And now in the Stillwater Jail I lie, a-wearin' my life away,
Two James boys live to tell the tale of that sad and fatal day.

Courtesy, Colorado Historical Society

Sam Bass

Sam Bass was born in In-di-an-a, it was his na-tive home, And at the age of sev-en - teen, young Sam be-gan to roam. He first came out to Tex-as,_____ a cow-boy for to be; A kind - er heart - ed fel-low_____ you sel - dom ev - er see.

Sam used to deal in race stock, one called the Denton mare,
He matched her in scrub races and took her to the Fair.
Sam used to coin the money and spent it just as free,
He always drank good whisky wherever he might be.

Sam left the Collins ranch in the merry month of May
With a herd of Texas cattle the Black Hills for to see,
Sold out in Custer City and then got on a spree –
A harder set of cowboys you seldom ever see.

On their way back to Texas they robbed the U. P. train.
And then split up in couples and started out again.
Joe Collins and his partner were overtaken soon,
With all their hard-earned money they had to meet their doom.

Sam made it back to Texas all right side up with care;
Rode into the town of Denton, with all his friends to share.
Sam's life was short in Texas; three robberies he did do,
He robbed all the passengers, mail and express cars too.

Sam had four companions – four bold and daring lads –
They were Richardson, Jackson, Joe Collins and Old Dad;
More bold and daring cowboys the Rangers never knew –
They whipped the Texas Rangers and ran the Boys in Blue.

Sam had another companion, called Arkansas for short,
Was shot by a Texas Ranger by the name of Thomas Floyd;
Oh, Tom is a big six-footer and thinks he's mighty fly,
But I can tell you his racket - he's a deadbeat on the sly.

Jim Murphy was arrested and then released on bail;
He jumped his bond at Tyler and then took the train for Terrell;
But Mayor Jones had posted Jim and that was all a stall,
'Twas only a plan to capture Sam before the coming Fall.

Sam met his fate at Round Rock, July the twenty-first.
They pierced poor Sam with rifle balls and emptied out his purse.
Poor Sam he is a corpse now and six feet under clay,
And Jackson's in the bushes trying to get away.

Jim had borrowed Sam's good gold and didn't want to pay;
The only shot he saw was to give poor Sam away.
He sold out Sam and Barnes and left their friends to mourn,
Oh, what a scorching Jim will get when Gabriel blows his horn.

And so he sold out Sam and Barnes and left their friends to mourn.
Oh, what a scorching Jim will get when Gabriel blows his horn.
Perhaps he's got to Heaven, there's none of us can say,
But if I'm right in my surmise he's gone the other way.

Jesse James

Jes-se James was a lad who __ killed man-y a man, He robbed the Glen – dale train. He __ stole from the rich and he gave to the poor, He'd a hand and a heart and a brain. Poor Jes-se had a wife to mourn for his life, Three chil – dren they were brave; But that

dirt-y lit-tle cow-ard who shot Mis-ter How-ard, has laid poor Jes-se in his grave.

It was Robert Ford, that dirty little coward,
I wonder how he does feel.
For he ate of Jesse's bread and he slept in Jesse's bed,
And he laid poor Jesse in his grave. *Chorus*

How the people held their breath when they heard of Jesse's death,
And wondered how he ever came to die.
It was one of the gang, called Little Robert Ford
That shot poor Jesse on the sly. *Chorus*

Jesse was a man, a friend to the poor,
He never would see a man suffer pain.
And with his brother Frank he robbed the Chicago bank,
And stopped the Glendale train. *Chorus*

It was on a Wednesday night, the moon was shining bright,
They stopped the Glendale train.
And the people, they did say for many miles away,
It was robbed by Frank and Jesse James. *Chorus*

They went to a crossing not very far from there,
And there they did the same.
With the agent on his knees, he delivered up the keys
To the outlaws, Frank and Jesse James. *Chorus*

It was on a Saturday night, Jesse was at home,
Talking to his family brave.
Robert Ford came along like a thief in the night
And laid poor Jesse in his grave. *Chorus*

This song was made by Billy Gashade
As soon as the news did arrive.
He said there was no man with the law in his hand
Who could take Jesse James while alive. *Chorus*

Courtesy, Colorado Historical Society

East Colorado Blues

This is the hammer that killed John Henry,
But it won't kill me.   (3)

Well, John Henry he left his hammer,
Lyin' side the road.   (3)

This old hammer fallin' from my shoulder,
The steel goin' down.   (3)

When you hear my hammer ringin',
Steel runnin' like lead.   (3)

Take this hammer, carry it to the captain,
Yes, tell him I'm gone.   (3)

Repeat first verse

A Cowboy's Life

A cow-boy's life is a wea-ry, drear-y life, Some say it's free from care; Round-ing up the cat-tle from morn-ing till night, In the mid-dle of the prai-rie so bare.

Half past four, the noisy cook will roar,
"Whoop-a-whoop-a-hey!"
Slowly you will rise with sleepy-feeling eyes,
The sweet dreamy night has passed away.

The wolves and owls with their terrifying howls
Disturb us in our midnight dream,
As we lie on our slickers in a cold, rainy night,
Way over on the Pecos stream.

Spring-time sets in, double trouble will begin,
The weather is so fierce and cold.
Our clothes are wet and frozen to our necks
And the cattle we can scarcely hold.

The cowboy's life is a dreary, dreary life,
He's driven through the heat and cold,
While the rich man's a-sleeping on his velvet couch,
A-dreaming of his silver and his gold.

The Texas Rangers

Come all you Tex-as Ran-gers, wher-ev-er you may

be, I hope you'll pay at-ten-tion, and

lis-ten un-to me. My name is noth-ing ex-

try, the truth to you I'll tell; I____

am a rov - ing Ran - ger, and I'm sure I wish you well.

'Twas at the age of sixteen I joined this jolly band,
We marched from San Antonio unto the Rio Grande,
Our captain, he informed us, perhaps he thought it right,
"Before you reach the station, boys, I'm sure you'll have to fight."

I saw the Injuns coming, I heard them give a yell,
My feelings at this moment no human tongue can tell,
I saw their glittering lances and their arrows 'round me flew,
And all my strength it left me and all my courage, too.

We fought full nine hours before the strife was o'er,
The like of dead and wounded I never saw before,
And when the sun was rising and the Indians they had fled,
We loaded up our rifles and counted up our dead.

Now all of us were wounded, our noble captain slain,
The sun was shining sadly across the bloody plain.
Sixteen brave Rangers as ever roamed the West,
Were buried by their comrades with arrows in their breast.

'Twas then I thought of mother, who to me in tears did say,
"To you they are all strangers, with me you'd better stay."
I thought that she was childish and that she did not know,
My mind was fixed on ranging and I was bound to go.

I have seen the fruits of rambling, I know its hardships well,
I have crossed the Rocky Mountains, rode down the streets of Hell,
I have been in the great Southwest, where wild Apaches roam,
And I tell you from experience, you'd better stay at home.

When The Work's All Done This Fall

A group of jol - ly cow - boys, dis - cuss - ing plans at ease; Says
am an old cow - punch - er, and here I'm dressed in rags; I

one, "I'll tell you some - thing, boys, if you will lis - ten, please. I
used to be a tough one, yes, and

go on great big jags. But I have got a home, boys, a
go - ing back to Dix - ie, once

good one you all know, Al - though I have - n't seen it _____ since
more to see them all I'm going to see my moth - er when the

long,   long a - go.   I'm   work's all   done this   fall."

"After the round-up's over, after the shipping's done,
I am going right straight home, boys, ere all my money's gone.
I have changed my ways, boys, no more will I fall;
And I am going home, boys, when the work's all done this fall.
When I first left home, boys, my sweet mother for me cried,
Begged me not to go, boys, for me she would have died.
My mother's heart is breaking, breaking for me, that's all,
And with God's help I'll see her when the work's all done this fall."

That very night this cowboy went out to stand his guard;
The night was dark and cloudy and storming very hard;
The cattle they got frightened and rushed in wild stampede,
The cowboy tried to head them, riding at full speed.
While riding in the darkness so loudly did he shout,
Trying his best to head them and turn the herd about,
His saddle horse did stumble and on him did fall,
The poor boy won't see his mother when the work's all done this fall.

His body was so mangled the boys all thought him dead,
They picked him up so gently and laid him on a bed;
He opened wide his blue eyes and looking all around
He motioned to his comrades to sit near him on the ground.
"Boys, send my mother my wages, the wages I have earned,
For I am afraid, boys, my last steer I have turned.
I'm going to a new range, I hear my Master's call,
And I'll not see my mother when the work's all done this fall."

"Bill, you may have my saddle; George, you may take my bed;
Jack may have my pistol, after I am dead.
Boys, think of me kindly when you look upon them all,
For I'll not see my mother when the work's all done this fall."
Poor Charlie was buried at sunrise, no tombstone at his head,
Nothing but a little board and this is what it said,
"Charlie died at daybreak, he died from a fall,
The boy won't see his mother when the work's all done this fall."

The Tenderfoot

I thought one day that just for fun I'd see how cow-punch-ing was done, So when the round – ups had be-gun, I tack-led a cat – tle king. _____ Says he, "My fore - man's gone to town. He's at the Red Eye, his name is Brown. If you see him he'll

take   you down."   Says   I,   "That's   just   the   thing."_____

We started for the ranch next day;
Brown augured me most all the way;
He said that punching was only play,
That it was no work at all;
That all you had to do was ride;
'Twas only drifting with the tide.
The son of gun, oh how he lied;
He certainly had his gall.

They saddled me up an old gray hack,
With two set fasts on his back,
They padded him down with a gunny sack
And used my bedding all,
When I got on he left the ground,
Went up in the air and looked around,
While I came down and busted the ground;
And got one hell of a fall.

Sometimes my horse would buck and break
Across the prairie he would take,
As if running for a stake
It seemed to them but play,
Sometimes I couldn't catch them at all,
Sometimes my horse would slip and fall
And I'd shoot on like a cannon ball
Till the earth came up my way.

They picked me up and carried me in
And rubbed me down with an old stake-pin.
"That's the way they all begin,
You're doing swell," says Brown.
"And by the morning if you don't die
I'll give you another horse to try."
"Oh, say, can't I walk?" says I.
Says he, "Yep, back to town."

I've traveled up, I've traveled down,
I've traveled this country round and round;
I've lived in city, I've lived in town,
And I've got this much to say:
Before you try cowpunching kiss your wife
Take heavy insurance on your life,
Then cut your throat with a carving knife,
It's easier to die that way.

Bury Me Not On The Lone Prairie

"Oh, bury me not on the lone prairie,
Where the wild coyotes will howl o'er me,
In a narrow grave just six by three.
Oh, bury me not on the lone prairie."

"It matters not, I've oft been told,
Where the body lies when the heart grows cold.
Yet grant, oh grant this wish to me:
Oh, bury me not on the lone prairie."

"I've always wished to be laid when I died
In the little churchyard on the green hillside.
By my father's grave there let mine be,
And bury me not on the lone prairie."

"Oh, bury me not" — and his voice failed there,
But we took no heed of his dying prayer.
In a narrow grave just six by three,
We buried him there on the lone prairie.

And the cowboys now as they roam the plain,
For they marked the spot where his bones were lain,
Fling a handful of roses o'er his grave,
With a prayer to Him who his soul will save.

The Streets Of Laredo

"I see by your outfit that you are a cowboy,"
These words he did say as I boldly walked by.
"Come sit down beside me and hear my sad story,
I'm shot in the breast and I know I must die.

"It was once in the saddle I used to go dashing,
Once in the saddle I used to go gay;
First down to Rosie's and then to the card-house —
Got shot in the breast and I'm dying today.

"Get sixteen gamblers to carry my coffin,
Let six jolly cowboys come sing me a song.
Take me to the graveyard and lay the sod o'er me,
For I'm a young cowboy and I know I've done wrong.

"Oh, beat the drum slowly and play the fife lowly,
Play the dead march as you carry me along.
Put bunches of roses all over my coffin,
Roses to deaden the clods as they fall."

Repeat first verse

Little Old Sod Shanty On The Plain

I'm look – ing rath – er seed – y now while hold – ing down my claim, And my vit – tles are not al – ways of the best.____

And the mice play shy – ly 'round me as I nes – tle down to
see the hun – gry coy - ote as he sneaks up through the

rest ⎱
grass ⎰ In my lit – tle old sod shan – ty on the plain.____

Fine

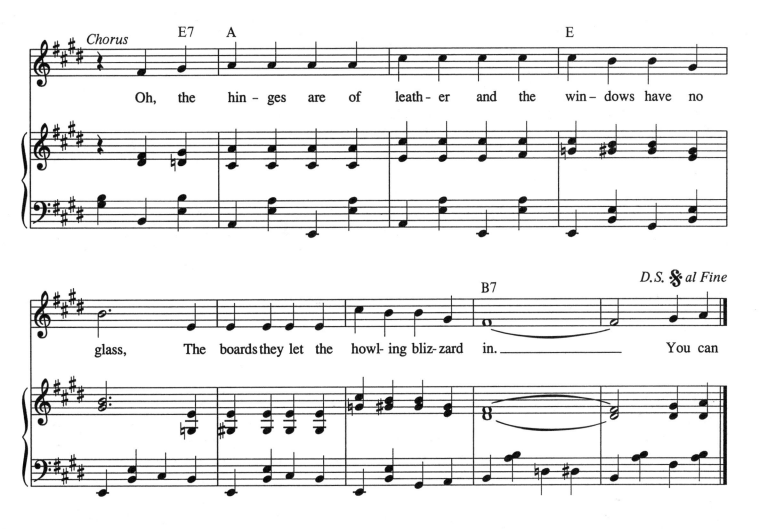

I rather like the novelty of living in this way,
Though my bill of fare isn't always of the best,
But I'm happy as a clam on the land of Uncle Sam,
In my little old sod shanty in the West. *Chorus*

But when I left my Eastern home, a bachelor so gay,
To try and win my way to wealth and fame,
I little thought I'd come down to burning twisted hay
In the little old sod shanty on my claim. *Chorus*

My clothes are plastered o'er with dough, I'm looking like a fright,
And everything is scattered 'round the room;
But I wouldn't give the freedom that I have out in the West
For the table of the Eastern man's old home. *Chorus*

Still, I wish that some kind-hearted girl would pity on me take,
And relieve me from the mess that I am in;
The angel, how I'd bless her if this her home she'd make
In the little old sod shanty on my claim! *Chorus*

And if fate should bless us with now and then an heir
To cheer our hearts with honest pride of fame,
Oh, then we'd be contented for the toil that we had spent
In the little old sod shanty on our claim. *Chorus*

When time enough had lapsed and all those little brats
To noble man and womanhood had grown,
It wouldn't seem half so lonely as 'round us we should look,
And we'd see the old sod shanty on our claim. *Chorus*

Starving To Death On A Government Claim

Chorus
Hurray for Greer County! the land of the free,
The land of the bedbug, grasshopper and flea;
I'll sing of its praises, I'll tell of its fame,
While starving to death on my government claim.

My house, it is built of national soil,
Its walls are erected according to Hoyle,
Its roof has no pitch, but is level and plain,
I always get wet if it happens to rain.   *Chorus*

My clothes are all ragged, as my language is rough,
My bread is corndodgers, both solid and tough;
But yet I am happy and live at my ease
On sorghum, molasses,bacon and cheese.   *Chorus*

How happy am I when I crawl into bed,
A rattlesnake hisses a tune at my head,
A gay little centipede, all without fear,
Crawls over my pillow and into my ear.   *Chorus*

Now all you claim holders, I hope you will stay
And chew your hardtack till you're toothless and gray,
But for myself I'll no longer remain
To starve like a dog on my government claim.   *Chorus*

Goodbye to Greer County where blizzards arise,
Where the sun never sinks and the flea never dies,
And the wind never ceases but always remains
Till it starves us all out on our government claims.   *Chorus*

Farewell to Greer County, farewell to the west,
I'll travel back east to the girl I love best.
I'll travel to Texas and marry me a wife,
And quit corn dodgers the rest of my life. *Chorus*

For Kansas

All who want to roam in Kan - sas, All who want to roam in Kan - sas, All who want to roam, go and get your-self a home, Be con-tent - ed with your doom in Kan - sas.

O the girls they do grow tall in Kansas, (2)
The girls they do grow tall and the boys
  they love them all,
And they marry 'em in the fall in Kansas.

The potatoes they grow small in Kansas, (2)
The potatoes they grow small and they
  dig them in the fall,
And they eat them tops and all in Kansas.

O they chew tobacco thin in Kansas, (2)
O they chew tobacco thin and it
  dribbles on their chin
And they lick it back again in Kansas.

Blood On The Saddle

Slowly, with great pathos

There was blood on the sad - dle, And blood on the ground, And a great big pud-dle ___ Of blood all a - round.

Oh, the cowboy lay in it
All covered with gore,
And he won't go a-riding
His bronco no more.

Oh, pity the cowboy
All bloody and red —
His bronco fell on him
And mashed in his head.